W9-ASV-504

Friends in Focus

By the same author

A PACIFIST'S WAR
MEMORIES
JULIA
EVERYTHING TO LOSE

Friends in Focus
A Life in Photographs

Frances Partridge

Chatto & Windus
LONDON

Published in 1987 by
Chatto & Windus Ltd,
30 Bedford Square,
London WC1B 3RP

All rights reserved. No part of this publication
may be reproduced, stored in a retrieval system, or
transmitted in any form, or by any means, electronic,
mechanical, photocopying, recording or otherwise,
without the prior permission of the publisher.

British Library Cataloguing in Publication Data

Partridge, Frances
Friends in focus: a life in photographs.
1. Partridge, Frances – Portraits
2. Pacifists – Great Britain – Biography
I. Title
327.1'72'0924   JX1962.P29

ISBN 0-7011-3229-9

Copyright © Frances Partridge 1987

Designed by Humphrey Stone

Photoset in Linotron Sabon by
Rowland Phototypesetting Ltd,
Bury St Edmunds, Suffolk
Printed in Great Britain by
Butler and Tanner Ltd,
Frome, Somerset

Introduction

In the bedroom of my London flat stands a tall solid old French cupboard, bought by Lytton Strachey more than sixty years ago and shipped to England from Provence; now mine. A lovely and lovable object, its outside is polished like a horsechestnut, and inside it is still lined with very old calendered chintz patterned in red and white. Its four shelves have for a long time contained my archives – letters, diaries, and eighteen photograph albums. It is a dossier of my life.

Whence comes this impulse to record the passing years? I suspect that more people than not belong to the squirrel tribe and simply love to collect around them objects which revive happy moments in their lives; nor is there any need to look further for a motive. I have never yet come across anyone who kept a book of disasters – sad portraits of their children receiving news of failure in their exams, disappointed travellers arriving at hideous foreign villas recklessly ordered by post, or standing forlornly on platforms after missing trains. So that a family album tends to exude an aroma of exaggerated happiness. But selective albums are not unknown. I have seen a hilariously entertaining one kept by Molly MacCarthy, wife of Desmond, which was devoted entirely to clergymen. Others have been confined to racehorses, actresses and so on.

We are all to some extent egotists, and just as egotism fuels the energy that drives the diarist's hand relentlessly across the page, it is behind the click of the photographer's shutter, though for obvious reasons less exclusively so. A lady at a cocktail party who had kindly mentioned my having published some extracts from my diaries went on to say rather fiercely: 'But why do you always write about *yourself*? *I* couldn't.' Here, at least, the photographer can claim an advantage: his eye is focused on the outer world, while the diarist looks inwards. But diary and camera share one great virtue. Merely to possess them sharpens the eyes and ears of their owner, intensifies his power to notice an expression changing a face, or the shadow of a cloud crossing a hill, which might otherwise have slipped by unobserved.

However, for most of us, and certainly for me, the photograph album is an arena wherein to oppose the hectic flight of Time and give a boost to the rickety vehicle of memory, overburdened as it is with heterogeneous images, valued for different reasons. For everything we do is governed by Time; one doesn't need to be old to appreciate its relentless march. I have recalled elsewhere how my son Burgo took against it at the age of five and a half, and said in a voice of horror: 'We can't stop the days coming. Even up in the sky and down in Devonshire and in France they still go on.' Perhaps our enjoyment of photograph albums comes partly from the fact that youth is preserved in them in the only possible sense. However, of course the friends in my albums lose their grace; their heads turn white, their faces become wrinkled. It would be very terrible if they didn't, and my collection much duller. I remember once being briefly haunted by the fantastic speculation that we might suddenly all begin growing *younger* instead of older. I passed it on to David Garnett as we sat outside his stone cottage in the Lot. A convulsion of amusement passed across his rosy septuagenarian face, and he hurried indoors, to return a few minutes later wearing a highly incongruous curly brown wig. 'Just to show you what it would be like if we all started growing younger,' he said. I wish I had had my camera with me.

Even without returning to the cavemen and their bisons, or even the Bayeux tapestry, we can't fail to realise that the recording impulse is as old as Man. It seems to me more extraordinary that its technical proficiency has developed so little in some cases – since the cave-paintings for instance – and in others to such an astonishing degree. (Just compare the harsh roaring that was Tennyson declaiming the *Charge of the Light*

Brigade into the earliest form of phonograph with the voices of long-dead singers as they now melt flawlessly into the atmosphere, and no pin drops.)

Most early photograph albums are depressing collections of thick oblongs of yellowish cardboard on which aunts and whiskered grandfathers seem to have been pressed like naturalists' specimens, standing stiffly among columns and swags of curtain, their fixed expressions probably due to the long time then needed to take a photograph. Today, by way of innovators like Julia Cameron, we have reached the other extreme, when every parent or traveller is equipped with a conveniently small machine, so simple (or perhaps I should say so complicated) that it makes decisions itself as to focus and 'aperture', turns on a flash when required and will even speak to the photographer in a midget's voice should he so desire. Package tours fairly bristle and crackle like popcorn with objects such as these. Perfect colour, whether in natural or artificial light is of course an irresistible and magic addition. (I am sometimes uncertain of its advantage and hanker for the austere emphasis of black and white.)

Selecting from my eighteen volumes has been no easy task. Although I have tried to make it my autobiography in pictures, it includes three volumes that were not mine. One belonged to Lytton Strachey. He bought an excellent second-hand camera which took postcard-size pictures when he managed to hold it straight or when it was seized upon by Carrington. Two books were hers. As the earliest, these three volumes are of most historical interest, and include characters such as Mark Gertler, Ottoline Morrell and Aldous Huxley, but many have suffered the fate of old photographs and faded to a dingy yellow, while others are hardly bigger than postage stamps. Mercifully, modern technique of enlargement and intensification has helped to rescue a representative number from oblivion. For although this album is designed to represent my own life, a considerable part of it – that is to say, after I became an adult – fell within the same sphere as Lytton Strachey's and Dora Carrington's lives, mine becoming for some years entangled with theirs, my friends being many of them chosen from the same world, my values being permanently affected by theirs, a state of things which continued after both their premature deaths, and has lasted until the present day. In that sense only can this be called a Bloomsbury album.

Naturally my friends, husband and son dominate the scene; but the passage of Time has also taken me 'down to Devonshire, to France' and other countries, and I have chosen some houses, places, groups and scenes that seemed to have intrinsic interest whether evocative or even sometimes comic. I have added comments and explanations according to what appeared individually desirable. In fact I have thoroughly enjoyed myself, and can only hope that in doing so I have given some entertainment.

1. I start my photographic autobiography with a few glimpses of my own prehistory. Of the six of us Marshalls two were boys – my brother Horace is on the right, a remote but kindly figure over six feet tall, and Tom, engaging and clever, in the middle. My two elder sisters, Judy, and Ray (who was to marry David Garnett and become the Lady into Fox) are on the left. Eleanor and myself, 'the little ones', wearing our best tussore silk frocks, are in front.

2. At ten I was beginning to find life
extraordinarily interesting.

OPPOSITE
3. Even more so at eighteen, when I went up to Newnham,
Cambridge, in 1918. Here I am walking to Trumpington,
snapped by a girlfriend

3

5

4. The First World War over, I began taking holidays abroad, rucksack on back, in the Dolomites perhaps. In a modest way I shared the passion some of my father's family felt for mountains. To me, the thrilling thing about alpine peaks was the way they lost their arrogant menace as one climbed, and changed their aspect with every step.

5. Meanwhile what of the others with whom my life was soon to become involved? Ralph Partridge was fishing with his Christ Church friend and fellow-oar Noel Carrington, while (6) his wartime friend Gerald Brenan was flirting with his wife, Noel's sister Dora, always known as Carrington. These photographs were probably taken at Watendlath in Cumberland in about 1921.

6

7

7. Ralph in rowing togs.

8. A firm friendship between Ralph and Lytton Strachey – seen here walking together in France – was the final link in the trio which settled into (9) Tidmarsh Mill House, near Pangbourne.

8

9

10. Garsington Manor was not far away from Tidmarsh and visits were often exchanged. Here is Lady Ottoline Morrell walking in her beautiful garden with Mark Gertler the painter, T. S. Eliot, and Juliette Huxley (who had come from Switzerland to help educate Julian, daughter of the house, and stayed to become Mrs Julian Huxley). The two Huxley brothers were frequent visitors.

11. I visited Ottoline in her panelled room painted Pompeian red. It was a house unlike any other I had seen, with its modern paintings, rich stuffs and amorous pug dogs. Ottoline is presiding here in an elaborate silk confection flowing to the ground, to give tea to Gertler and Eliot.

12. It's hard to guess what frolicsome impulse had made the deeply serious Aldous Huxley join hands with his sister-in-law and Mark Gertler in a round dance, but acting – like dressing up – belonged very much to the spirit of the age.

13. After one or two professional calls at Birrell and Garnett's bookshop, where I was working, Ralph invited me to spend a weekend at Tidmarsh in 1923. I was very shy, and it was not altogether a success. Walking over this bridge are Ralph, E. M. Forster (in his inevitable cloth cap), Lytton, a rather *louche* French doctor, and myself. That evening, after offering Ralph what he called 'rotten addresses' in various towns, the doctor suggested a paper game – we should all write on bits of paper how and when we had lost our virginities. I felt too embarrassed and ashamed to write 'Never'!

13

14

14. Carrington and her friend, Barbara Bagenal, were among the first Slade students to cut their hair short. Virginia Woolf christened them the 'cropheads'. Perhaps she was critical of them at times, but she showed sensitive kindness to both when they were in trouble.

15. In 1924 came the move from Tidmarsh to
Ham Spray House on the borders of Berkshire and
Wiltshire. Its early-Victorian front had been
spotted and fallen in love with during a walk
along the downs to Inkpen Gibbet. Lytton and
Ralph bid for it against a rich rival who was
fortunately too mean to go above £2000. There
was much cutting down of trees, and painting
and papering the interior. Here is the dining room.
Carrington painted the dresser with motifs from
Rouen ware, and we covered it with Spanish
pottery and English lustre. The pictures were by
Duncan Grant and Carrington.

16. Carrington joins Lytton on the lawn before saddling her white pony, Belle, and going for a ride on the downs.

17. Meals were eaten in the garden as often as possible. Two of Lytton's favourite young friends, George (Dadie) Rylands and Rosamond Lehmann are having tea with him.

18. Lytton always kept his close connection with Cambridge. Having bought a second-hand camera, he took it with him on a visit to Dadie, who was an ideal subject.

19

20

19. Two other Cambridge posers were J. T. Sheppard, later Sir John and Provost of King's, and (20) Goldsworthy Lowes Dickinson, historian and philosophical writer. They make an interesting pair, the one ebullient, the other a little sombre, a difference also perhaps expressed in the contrasting folds of their trousers.

21. Among these undergraduates bathing and boating are Anthony Blunt, later Director of the Courtauld and Keeper of the Queen's Pictures, Francis Warre Cornish, Dadie Rylands and Eddie (later Sir Edward) Playfair.

21

22. Another famous Cambridge character dating from an earlier period was Saxon Sydney-Turner, who figures in all Bloomsbury memoirs, and spent his whole life working in the Treasury. A frequent visitor to Ham Spray almost until his death, he is standing with me at the garden door.

23. Each of Ham Spray's denizens had their own particular friends and relations. Lady Strachey must do duty for the whole family including all those of her children and grandchildren who do *not* appear in this album, for they were as close-knit as any Scottish clan. The force of her personality and intelligence is plainly seen in the position of her left hand.

24. Brian Howard, successfully snapped by Lytton's camera. He was remarkable for literary talent, personal brio, and enormous eyes.

25. But Roger Senhouse became Lytton's favourite. He had a character of great sweetness, perfect good looks, irresistible charm – and scant respect for the truth.

26

27

26. The John family made up an important part of Carrington's world. She had long been a friend of Augustus, who is seen here on the deck of the trawler *Sanspareil* with her master Bernard (Beakus) Penrose, whose bright blue eyes and sculptured bronzed features made him the very image of a sailor. As is well known, he was the object of Carrington's last attachment, and she too sometimes went sailing with him. Beakus planned many voyages but seldom took to sea, and it was maliciously said that he really preferred to put up in a pub in Brixham harbour, whence he would give a shout now and again of '*Sanspareil* ahoy!'

27. Dorelia John was also much admired by Carrington, and indeed everyone else. How could she not be, with beauty, good taste and talent in making a garden, cooking and decorating her house? She spoke in a low husky voice, was sparing with words, and liked playing Bach on the piano.

28. Dorelia's two pretty daughters, Poppet and Vivien, appear here in their early teens, high-spirited and enthusiastic. With them are the painter Henry Lamb and the lovely Lady Pansy (*née* Pakenham), not long after their marriage.

28

29. Some visitors to Ham Spray were equally popular with everyone. Julia Strachey had been my 'best friend' since we were eight and nine, and was a great favourite of Carrington's also. She had recently begun earning her living as a model to Poiret in Paris, but her outfit in this picture, and her Eton crop, are more in the style of Chanel. She was seldom to be seen without a kitten or two.

29

30. Iris Tree, glamorous poetess and daughter of Sir Herbert Beerbohm Tree, with Lytton.

30

31. Boris Anrep, lifelong visitor to Ham Spray, and a glorious companion. The greatest of modern mosaicists, he came to England from Russia after the 1917 revolution.

32. Tommy Earp's expressive face and high surprised voice made one laugh as soon as he opened his mouth. There was a rumour that he had once been a rich *bon vivant* with long hair; but he was now a hard-up art critic who wore his hair very short *en brosse*, and delighted everyone by his special brand of wit.

33. Peter Morris and Mary Hutchinson, Lytton's cousin and confidante, who used modestly to describe herself as *une belle laide* despite her obvious attractions. She was for many years the love of Clive Bell.

32

31

33

34. Arthur Waley, distinguished orientalist and translator, was also remarkable for his impassivity both of expression and speech. I used to go to a skating rink with him, and discovered that even a tangled fall on the ice when waltzing left his calm completely unshattered.

35. Sebastian Sprott, socio-psychologist, well-known Cambridge character, and great friend of Lytton and Maynard Keynes; Gerald Heard, guru; and E. M. Forster, breakfasting on the lawn with Lytton.

34

35

36. Raymond Mortimer posing as Saint Sebastian against our dartboard.

37. The marriage between Julia Strachey and Stephen (Tommy) Tomlin, two talented neurotics – one a writer, the other a sculptor – was devised by Carrington but could not be called a success.

38. Myself at our bathing-place, a backwater of the river Kennet.

39

39. There were many contacts with the Bell family
and Duncan Grant, most often at Charleston,
but sometimes at their house at Cassis in the Midi.
Lytton took this snapshot of Vanessa and
Duncan when visiting them there from his sister
Dorothy Bussy's house at Roquebrune.

40. A large and cheerful weekend at Charleston in 1928. From left to right are myself, Quentin and Julian, Duncan, Clive and his friend Beatrice (Bobo) Mayor, a playwright; Roger Fry and Raymond Mortimer in front.

41

42

43

41. Virginia Woolf and Quentin very much
enjoyed each other's company; dark though this
photograph is, it conveys Virginia's mysterious
fascination and I value it as the only one I took
of her myself.

42. It was usually Clive who invited me to
Charleston, but for Ralph as well as me he was a
valued friend. Francis (Frankie) Birrell had been
joint owner of my bookshop with Bunny Garnett.
He was a happy character who spread
his happiness to everyone around him, and (43) was
always ready to act in a Charleston performance
of Molière, say, along with Angelica and her friends.

44. More play-acting: Eve Disher (painter) and
Angus Davidson (writer and translator from Italian,
who often sat to Duncan and Vanessa) are posing
for 'The Proposal'.

44

45

45. Bryan and Diana Guinness were neighbours over the downs. Diana (now Lady Mosley) has written of her affection for Lytton and Carrington, which was warmly returned.

46. Maynard and Lydia Keynes were all too infrequent visitors.

47. Lytton remained devoted to Roger until the end of his life.

46

48

49

48. 1926 was the year of change at Ham Spray. Ralph and I set up our own separate establishment in Gordon Square, although we still came very often to Ham Spray. We also took several trips abroad – to Corsica, for instance, where a friendly dog has joined our bathe in a mountain stream.

49. That year we went to stay with Gerald Brenan for the first time in his mountain fastness at Yegen. It took us four days and nights to get there in those pre-aeroplane days, and our journey ended on mules in the darkness, at an altitude of 4000 feet. Next morning we were confronted by a sensational view.

50. This was the village street beneath his window, into which Gerald once threw his midday *tortilla*, plate and all, because it wasn't to his liking. No traffic except mules could reach the village, for the simple reason that there was no road.

51. We explored other neighbouring villages, and brought back the old Spanish plates and jugs which the inhabitants were eager to sell. Here I am sharing a mule with Gerald's girl-friend, Juliana, while he leads us.

52. Of the four Penrose brothers – Alec, Lionel, Roland and Beakus – Lionel, the brilliant geneticist, and his wife Margaret were the ones Ralph and I saw most of. Margaret was clever also, and all their children exceptionally so; their youngest son Jonathan was English chess champion for ten years running.

53. Our dear friend Maroussa Volkova was Boris Anrep's 'consort', in character and appearance dramatically Russian. We saw them often in London, sometimes at their studio in Hampstead. Later on, especially during and after the Second World War, they were favourite guests at Ham Spray.

54. One weekend at Ham Spray was given over to acting a home-made film called *Dr Turner's Mental Home*, with Beakus Penrose as cameraman. Rachel MacCarthy (later Lady David Cecil) was the leading lady, and took the part of a young girl wrongly incarcerated by the wicked doctor, brilliantly played by Saxon Sydney-Turner who enjoyed himself hugely. She is posing here in the bath outside the greenhouse.

55. Ralph and I sometimes stayed in Suffolk with Roger Fry and Helen Anrep (Boris's wife but now virtually married to Roger). This meant a lot of chess with Roger, and much enjoyable talk. Roger had the Old Bloomsbury love of general ideas and 'going into' every subject, but was also fond of gossip and talk in a lighter vein.

54

55

56

57

56. In summer we went swimming with Carrington's brother Noel and his wife Catharine. In hard winters we skated on the frozen Kennet canal.

57. At Cambridge we used to visit my old schoolfriend Lettice Baker and her husband, the brilliant young philosopher Frank Ramsey. Here they are walking beside the Cam to meet us, with Elizabeth Denby. Frank's death before he was thirty was a major tragedy.

58. Lytton had been delicate as child and man. In the autumn of 1931 he developed alarming symptoms and took to his bed in the care of nurses, as well as Carrington of course and many of his Strachey relations. After agonisingly anxious weeks he died in January 1932. Carrington – as she copied in her diary – 'for a little tried, To live without him, liked it not and died' in March.

59

60

59. Stricken by this double tragedy, Ralph and I took refuge briefly with the Brenans – for Gerald was now married to Gamel Woolsey – in Dorset; and afterwards (60) in driving through the battlefields of France. Ralph hoped that by reviving the memories of past horrors he might distract his mind from present grief. We were appalled and amazed that so many scars of 1914–18 remained. Here we are visiting the family with whom he was billetted at Oosthof in Flanders.

61. When we returned to England there was never any question of living anywhere but Ham Spray. Our friends rallied round us there, among them David Cecil and Rachel MacCarthy, who had recently embarked on the happiest of marriages.

62. Wogan and Rosamond Philipps came to feed the pigeons during one of Saxon's visits.

61

62

63

64

63. Quentin arrived in his dungarees with a small bag of painting materials. He worked hard and swam in our newly-built pool.

64. Though many of our friends were musical, few were instrumentalists. However, Dermod MacCarthy, doctor son of Desmond and Molly, played both flute and guitar.

65. Ralph and I had always liked reading different books in close proximity; here we are on a visit to Suffolk.

66

66. Early in 1933 Ralph and I got married and took ship for Southern Spain, heading inevitably for Yegen. We are at luncheon here with Gamel, waited on by 'White Maria', in the Granero, the main sitting-room of Gerald's cottage.

67. When not out walking, most of the day was spent on the terrace, where Gamel is sitting. Gamel came from South Carolina. Gerald had met her with the literary Powys family, and she too was a writer, mainly of poetry.

68. Back to Ham Spray's welcoming face, and to receive James and Alix Strachey, who made a habit of spending a much-enjoyed week with us every summer. Perhaps none of our visitors seemed more like 'family'.

69. Adrian Stephen, brother of Vanessa and Virginia – a distinguished-looking six-foot-six.

70. The sausage advertisement on Hungerford Station had a brazen, English charm. I posed Sydney Sheppard in front of it, whereas (71) his wife Clare, Rachel Cecil's cousin, appears as a genuine Essex mudlark. Both are sculptors.

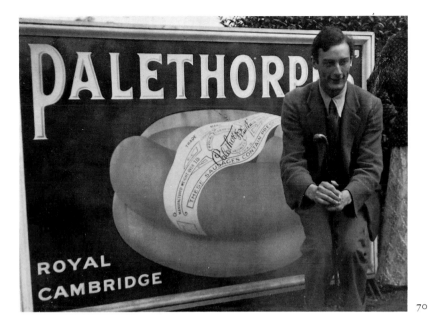

70

71

72

73

72. Dermod pours out after-lunch coffee for himself and Eddie Gathorne-Hardy. Like many of his family Eddie was a botanist, and liked to come flower-hunting with me, but – being lazy as well as amusing, erudite, selfish and ribald – he preferred to be driven to within a few yards of the plant we were seeking.

73. Julian Bell and Alix liked to engage in long closely reasoned arguments, often about politics or general ideas. Julian was killed in the Spanish Civil War a year or two later.

74. The arrival of a piano and radiogram converted a rather unpopular north room into 'the music room'. Saxon and Frankie Birrell are having tea in its bow window. The pollarded trunk of the great aspen seen through the window was nearly always chock-full of barn owls.

75. Bowls was played all over the lawn, following rules of our own. Roger Senhouse, Alix and Ralph are playing, with James watching. There was a badminton court in summer, and we occasionally attempted croquet, but Raymond, who adored the game, said it 'was like trying to cut a steak with a tea-spoon'.

74

75

77

76. Rosamond taming one of the doves whose home was a wicker cage swinging among blowsy pink roses on the verandah. They looked so pretty there that we put up with their amorous cooing in the mating season, maddening though it was.

77. Lytton's nephew, John Strachey (painter) with his wife Isobel. She and I were each expecting our first child at the same time.

78. Burgo was the first to arrive, and Charlotte Strachey a month later. They were friends as children, and indeed throughout their all too short lives.

78

79. Among several friends within driving distance were the Cecils at Rockbourne, where there was much more fun and conversation than appears in this carefully posed group (Rachel, her brother Michael, and Bryan Guinness, later Lord Moyne).

80. Ham Spray was 600 feet up, and in winter cold mists sometimes kept us at home for days on end.

81. Ralph was an expert pruner of fruit trees; here he is giving a demonstration to the Lambs at Coombe Bisset.

81

82. Anthony Powell had already published several of his successful novels when he came for the weekend with his wife, Lady Violet.

82

83

83. Ralph teaching Burgo to walk, as – a few years later – he taught him to swim.

84. Romilly John, son of Augustus and Dorelia, his clever wife Kathy and myself. Both were writers and not entirely in tune with their parents' romantic bohemian life. Always together, they were sufficient to themselves. I remember them quoting whole pages of Jane Austen by heart.

85. We had first met Jan Woolley and her daughter Janetta in Spain, not long before the outbreak of the Spanish Civil War. Frighteningly caught between rival forces in Malaga, they returned home by sea with other English tourists, and for a while made Ham Spray their base. Janetta was about fifteen.

85

86

87

86. We travelled abroad once or twice most years. In 1937 Raymond tempted us to join him and his friend Paul Hyslop at Kitzbühl.

87. Ralph took to skiing and went again a year later, but once was enough for me.

88. A Hellenic cruise was much more to my taste. We went with the Cecils and David's father Lord Salisbury, travelling in an ancient Scottish boat, the *Letitia*, which fed us on smoked fish from Glasgow. Here we are landing at Taormina.

89. David posing on the throne of Minos at Knossos.

90. Mistra beat everywhere else for me. David and Rachel in the Cathedral.

91. On the way home we made a detour to Cassis to see the Woolleys, and met Janetta's brother Rollo.

92. Raymond, Ralph and Janetta enjoying themselves motoring in France.

91

92

93. Once a youthful appendage to Old Bloomsbury, Sebastian Sprott became a professor at Nottingham University, where he stayed despite tempting offers from his old university, Cambridge. For he was quite without ambition, though domestic, adaptable, interested in everyone and everything. He came to see us faithfully every autumn at Ham Spray and once in Spain.

94. John Banting, lovable and affectionate; his character was as surrealist as his brilliant paintings.

94

93

95. 'The loneliness of childhood' was the title given to this moving winter portrait of Burgo, while this one (96) was called 'The gloom of Christmas'. The company so dismally assembled consists of Saxon, Rollo and Janetta, and Julia Strachey.

95

96

97. Two of those who
figured more prominently in
our lives than they do in
this album are here
together in close and
charming amity: Helen
Anrep, wife of Boris but
consort of Roger Fry; and
Bunny Garnett, my
bookshop boss, my
brother-in-law and finally
my co-grandparent.

98. Raymond, Patrick (later Lord) Kinross – a relaxed-looking weekend group, although I remember that our party included *two* newly-married couples.

99. Dermod 'as Gandhi'.

100. Eddy Sackville-West, distinguished music-critic and writer, christened this picture of himself, Janetta and Burgo 'Music, Poetry and Innocence'. After the weekend Eddy wrote to me: 'I must say I was considerably moved by Janetta, as no doubt you noticed. I wish she would marry me.'

98

99

100

101. WAR. Our first refugees were Philip and Phyllis Nichols and their children Francis and Anne. Phyllis shared our pacifist beliefs, and those of Julia, who had also fled from London to the peace of Wiltshire. Philip, who was a diplomat and later an ambassador, did not; nor did my valiant old mother. So the house remained in a state of unarmed neutrality.

102. James Strachey making use of the idleness due to 'the refugee psychoanalysts from Vienna snapping up all the patients' to study Egyptian hieroglyphics.

103. Heywood Hill, founder of the famous bookshop in Curzon Street, awaits call-up at Ham Spray with his wife, Lady Anne, and Julia.

103

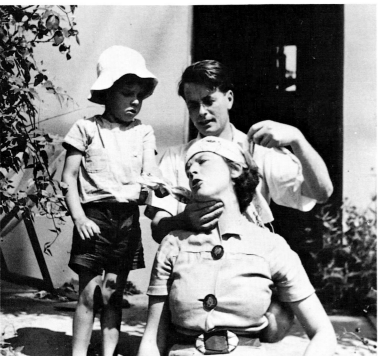

04

104. Burgo watches anxiously as the Hills do bandage practice in preparation for their first-aid class.

105

105. A visit from Desmond and Molly MacCarthy was
a great treat, although they usually forgot to
bring such things as their rations or batteries
for Molly's deaf-aid. Both were highly amusing
talkers, and Molly was not nearly so conventional as
she looks here.

106. January 1940 was fabulously cold. Iced pipes
and ice-enclosed trees were made up for by a
magic fortnight largely spent skating down the
Kennet canal.

107. Burgo shared his parents' love of cats. We
usually had two. This is Tiglath, or Tiger. Poor
Pileser had recently been shot by a gamekeeper.

108. PEACE: We celebrated it by a holiday with James and Alix on the shores of Lake Lugano. Burgo learned to crawl and dive, and (109) also to row. His great friend Vicky Strachey joined us at Ascona (110).

110

111. Home again, we were visited by our neighbours. Anthony West, son of H. G. Wells and Rebecca West, and his wife Kitty, the painter Katharine Church.

112. Others came from London for the weekend, like the Cochemés – Jacques, a biologist, and Joan, a painter.

113. Or we went visiting ourselves – for instance to Hilton Hall, near Cambridge, where I took this picture of the two eldest little Garnett girls, Amaryllis and Henrietta. Little did we think that Henrietta would one day become our daughter-in-law by marrying Burgo.

114. We made some new friends who were to play a large part in our lives. These were Robin and Lady Mary Campbell. Mary, Ralph and Ben Nicolson, the art historian, are seen here by the swimming pool.

115. A happy picture of Janetta with Robert Kee, whom she had married soon after his return from a tough war in the RAF and prison-camp.

116. A mutual understanding between Ralph and our new tabby kitten.

117. Ralph was commissioned to write a history and description of Broadmoor Criminal Lunatic Asylum, which led to many unforgettable visits and extraordinary experiences among the patients. He is with the 'Super', Dr Hopwood, and his spaniel, Crook.

118. During the summer holidays we took Burgo and Vicky on a trip to the Dordogne, sightseeing here at Chartres and at other places on our way across France.

118

119. It was very hot and the caves were cool. We all enjoyed hunting for prehistoric flints and bones.

119

120. Here is Kitty West painting our famous view
on a crisp winter's day.

121. Saxon had loved Barbara Bagenal for the whole of his life, and no one else, so far as is known. He wrote her a letter beginning 'Barbara!' every single day.

122. Quentin Bell and Olivier Popham after announcing that they were to marry. I would like to think the decision may have been reached at Ham Spray. I have spent more happy days than I can count with them in Sussex.

123. In the early Fifties we went in for a lot of foreign travel. Janetta's marriage to Robert Kee was at an end and she was now with Derek Jackson, scientist, rider in the Grand National and ex-wing-commander. We arranged to meet them and the Campbells in the small French town of Buis-les-Baronnies, where Janetta's mother, Jan, had spent part of the war. The tension of the occasion is possibly seen in this group of Janetta, Robin Campbell and Derek.

123

124. The Campbells at the Fountain of Vaucluse. 'He for God only, she for God in him', was one comment on this picture.

124

125. Again with the Campbells, we rented a collapsing Renaissance château at Menerbes in Provence. Ralph is sitting on the terrace with the Campbells and Mary's daughter, the writer Nell Dunn.

125

126

126. Three Partridges next took wing to Spain, taking Pippa Strachey, sister of Vicky, who is posing near the road to Granada.

127. Pippa, Ralph and Burgo, lunching at Jerez, after drinking far too many brands of sherry at the Bodega – a form of torment applied to visitors by the mocking staff.

127

128. During a few days in Portugal I took this splendid picture of the water garden at the episcopal palace of Castelo Branco. It seems to me too good to be excluded.

128

129. A remarkable piece of *gros-point* designed and being executed by Richard (Dicky) Chopping, novelist and flower-painter. I am sorry that the picture so effectually masks him.

130. When we spent our first weekend at Long Crichel House in Dorset, all four of our hosts were there. This is Eardley Knollys, painter, who made one of the original trio with Eddy Sackville-West and Desmond Shawe-Taylor. Raymond Mortimer joined them later.

131. Burgo didn't take kindly to boarding school, but after a somewhat stormy voyage he arrived safely at Ralph's old college, Christ Church.

131

132. My nephew Richard Garnett, a member of the firm of Macmillan's the publishers, with his wife Jane.

132

133. A touching father and daughter portrait – Robert Kee and Georgie, child of Janetta.

134. Ralph and I had never been to Italy together, and this was my first visit to Rome. On the Capitol we were unexpectedly accosted by Robert, pretending to be an Italian tout, and in our hotel, the *Inghilterra*, whom should we find but Henry and Pansy Lamb (135). I never knew more dedicated sightseers. They came with us on several trips – this, the longest, was to Urbino.

134

135

136. The verandah was the centre of much Ham Spray life. It was at its serenest when the weather was fine enough to breakfast there, as Janetta is doing in this picture.

136

137

137. Wynne and Kitty Godley sip sherry as they study our albums, in which are many other photographs of themselves.

138. We were delighted when Burgo brought two of his friends over from Oxford for the day. They were Simon Young and Harry Graham.

139

140

139. 1955 was a red-letter year, because during its summer one of our most ambitious and successful family holidays took place: along with Janetta we rented a large house in Galicia, Northern Spain, which we had never seen. It had belonged to a famous authority on El Greco. The journey from the village to our house was alarmingly dusty and full of potholes. I have allowed this holiday more coverage than usual.

140. What with Janetta's three little girls and monumental Nannie, three Partridges, not to mention a succession of visitors and the lady who had rented us the house but refused to leave it, we needed these three charming girls as servants. There were absolutely no modern conveniences and every drop of water had to be drawn from the well.

141. In the *comedor* are gathered Jonny Gathorne-Hardy, his cousin Caroline Jarvis (now the Countess of Cranbrook), Burgo, Janetta's Nicky, Ralph and Janetta.

142. Caroline is making the best of a hard floor, owing to chair shortage. She and Jonny had come straight from Cambridge.

143. The large attractive garden was a good place for me to cut Ralph's hair.

141

142

143

144. Our shopping town, Betanzos, was built in typical Galician style. People carried everything on their heads – even coffins.

145. A great deal of the days were spent on the splendid beaches. Desmond Shawe-Taylor, arriving from Portugal, helps Rose unravel a maze.

146. Burgo and Jonny playing beach games on the hard sand.

147. Nicky as a seaweed-clad mermaid.

148. Sometimes the wind from the Atlantic was uncomfortably strong.

149. A contrast in shapes – Rose's Nannie couldn't get over the strange ways and appearance of the natives.

144

145

150. Home again, we are visited by two of our brightest friends – Raymond Mortimer and V. S. Pritchett.

151. Lawrence Gowing telling a funny story, judging by the expressions of Burgo and Mary Campbell.

2

153

152. In 1956 Ralph's health began to intervene seriously in our lives. His first heart attack persuaded us to flee from English winter to the south of Spain. With enormous kindness, Bill and Annie Davis, hitherto complete strangers, invited us to stay while we found a house. Here is Bill, host of La Cónsula, with his guard dog.

153. Janetta had come out with us; together we found and moved into a nice little house near Gerald's. The Campbells were staying at La Cónsula; Mary and Janetta sunning themselves in our patio.

154. Ralph very much enjoyed choosing fish in Malaga market.

154

155. There were lunch picnics almost every day. Janetta and Ralph are in one of our favourite places – the Puerta de Leon on the road north, with its magnificent views.

156. Lunching with the Brenans at a Malaga fish restaurant.

157. This beach picnic was the occasion of our first getting to know Jaime Parladé, today Janetta's husband.

158. The happiest time in Gamel Brenan's day was spent feeding her cats.

157

158

159

161

160

16

159. Our Spanish winter had been a great success, but we were always pleased to be back on our verandah looking at the downs, like Georgie Kee, Janetta and Burgo.

160. A weekend away for a change, at Mottisfont, the fine old house of Maud Russell, close friend of Boris Anrep. He, Clive Bell and Ralph are with her in this picture.

161. Jonny Gathorne-Hardy and Anthony West.

162. A game of chess between Burgo and Anthony Blond, who had not only published his first book but (163) also married his childhood's friend Charlotte Strachey, who was as funny and charming as she was pretty. Our view makes a good back-drop for her.

164. Our second Spanish winter. Christmas Day
lunch was out of doors at La Cónsula, and even
the plentiful red wine failed to keep us warm. At
the table from left to right sit: an American guest,
Annie Davis, Ralph, Lord Weymouth, Joanna
Carrington (niece of Dora Carrington), Burgo,
Gamel, and, on the right, Hamish St Clair-Erskine.

165. We drove to the mountain villages near Yegen in search of carpets for sale. Woven from rags, they washed and wore splendidly. I have them still.

166. A picnic near the mountain village of Mijas gives some idea of how idyllic were the surroundings of that now spoiled village, once a centre of agate mines. Green hills dotted with olive groves rolled down to the sea. And this was midwinter! Here are Burgo, Ralph, Gerald and Joanna Carrington, who was staying with the Brenans, and whose likeness to her aunt Gerald had reacted to.

165

166

167

167. The arrival at La Cónsula of Annie's brother-in-law, Cyril Connolly, sent the red carpet rolling out, and we all took turns to invite him to lunch; at this Malaga restaurant he is with Annie and Ralph, and (168) here with Robin Campbell and Gamel.

169. Cyril 'in listening to music position' – Janetta's description of his manner of withdrawing from the company without actually leaving the room.

168

170. Jaime Parladé entertaining Janetta, Susan Benson (now Campbell) and Rosemary Strachey at his father's house Al CuzCuz, which is now his own and Janetta's.

171. Cyril and Anne Gage visiting us on our patio. He always complained if there was a shortage of pretty girls.

172. This year we drove home through Portugal, where we were visited in our hotel by Xan and Daphne Fielding.

173. An old Spanish peasant woman has decided Gerald needs a wigging – for what, I wonder?

174

174. Friends of the late Fifties are a mixture of old
and new, but the years take their toll. Eddy
Sackville-West has grown a beard. Peter Morris
and his sister Dora look older but still handsome.
Dora's husband Lord Romilly (Bunny) never
changes.

175. Philip Toynbee, Robin Campbell, Burgo and
I studying photograph albums with evident interest.

176. We had known Nicko Henderson (now Sir
Nicholas) since he was at his prep school. Since he
joined the Foreign Service, married Mary and
became ambassador to Poland, Germany, France
and USA, they have entertained us at several
capitals. Here they both are on our lawn, with
Robert Kee, one of Nicko's best friends at Oxford.

177. *Clematis montana* on our verandah makes a floriferous bower for Janetta and her children, and (178) for Georgie Kee and myself.

179. The Duchess of Devonshire gracing Ham Spray with her company during a bottling session of some Spanish wine. Robert and Ralph entertain her meanwhile.

180. Desmond and Raymond (in his 'pram', as it was called) on a fine summer day at Long Crichel.

181

181. A visit to Chatsworth. The Duke and Patrick Kinross look down from the terrace.

182. A new and always entertaining friend was brought to Ham Spray by Janetta – the writer Patrick Leigh Fermor.

183. One of our oldest and best loved friends, Boris Anrep, never seemed to change at all. He is sitting in the garden at Mottisfont with two comparatively new ones – Giana and Noel Blakiston, both writers.

182

187

184. As for Duncan Grant, seen here at Long Crichel with Eardley Knollys, he never looked a day older, at least until he was ninety.

185. There was sometimes more music than conversation in the Garnett's beautiful Queen Anne House near Cambridge. Bunny is sitting under a portrait of Angelica. My nephew William and Amaryllis are to the left and right.

186. Among a bevy of Garnett girls in the garden at Hilton, only one of the twins, Nerissa, is absent.

187. We always kept in touch with David and Rachel Cecil and their happy family. Visiting them at Cranborne one might find them all gathered. Here Lady Emma Cavendish stands in front of Hugh, David, Rachel, Jonathan and Laura.

188. Phil and Phyllis Nichols, our refugees at the start of the war, entertained us at the embassy at the Hague and in their Elizabethan house in Essex.

189. Two successive Heads of the Slade School – Sir Lawrence Gowing and Sir William Coldstream.

190. E. M. Forster must have outlived very many of his old friends, but he also made many new ones, including those who went to see him in his rooms at Cambridge. He is here at Long Crichel with one of these, Mattei Radev, expert picture-framer.

188

189

191. Clive was another dear old friend who changed very little. This portrait was taken with the painter Lindy Dufferin in the dining room at Charleston, and shows the original black hand-made wallpaper and the round table before they were restored.

192. Bunny and Angelica Garnett on Ham Spray verandah.

193. This was the last photograph I ever took of Ralph, on a visit to Alix and James Strachey at Marlow, with Angus Davidson.

194

194. Twenty-seven years have passed since the last
picture, but I propose to pursue my autobiography
no further, especially as I took at about this time
to colour photography. I shall sign off with a
genealogical CODA, covering that intervening
time. Burgo and Henrietta Garnett were married
in 1962.

195

195. Their daughter Sophie Vanessa was born in 1963.

196. In 1983 my granddaughter Sophie married Wenzel Gelpke in Tuscany, where they live and farm.

196

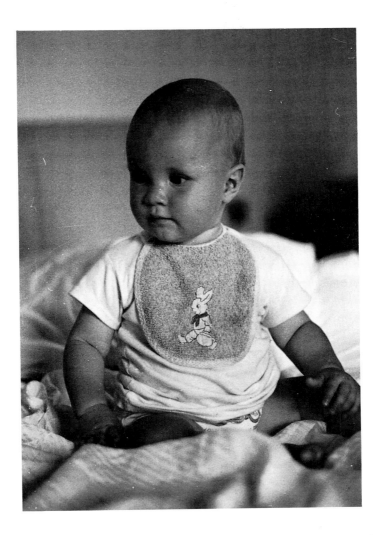

197. In 1985 my great-granddaughter,
Julia Frances, was born.